Healthy Eating

JANE SIEVING PELKKI

Children's Press®
An Imprint of Scholastic Inc.

Content Consultant
Phyllis Meadows, PhD, MSN, RN
Associate Dean for Practice, Clinical Professor, Health Management and Policy
University of Michigan, Ann Arbor, Michigan

Library of Congress Cataloging-in-Publication Data
Names: Pelkki, Jane Sieving, author.
Title: Healthy eating / by Jane Sieving Pelkki.
Other titles: True book.
Description: New York : Children's Press, an imprint of Scholastic Inc., [2016] | Series: A true book
Identifiers: LCCN 2015048496| ISBN 9780531228487 (library binding) | ISBN 9780531233306 (pbk.)
Subjects: LCSH: Nutrition—Juvenile literature. | Dietetics—Juvenile literature. | Health—Juvenile literature.
Classification: LCC TX355 .P35 2016 | DDC 613.2—dc23
LC record available at http://lccn.loc.gov/2015048496

Front cover: People preparing a salad

Back cover: A young girl with fruits and fruit juice

Find the Truth!

Everything you are about to read is true *except* for one of the sentences on this page.

Which one is **TRUE**?

T or F Today's Olympic athletes eat healthy because of discoveries made in the 1900s.

T or F It is never healthy to eat fat.

Find the answers in this book.

3

Contents

1 The Right Food

Can healthy eating make you
stronger and smarter?. **7**

2 The Building Blocks of Food

How do our bodies use food?. **11**

THE BIG TRUTH!

All Day

What's on the menu for a healthy eater?. . . . **22**

Even dessert
can be healthy
for you.

Oatmeal

3 Making Healthy Choices

How do you tell the difference between
healthy and unhealthy foods?............... **25**

4 The Science of Healthy Eating

How has our knowledge of
nutrition grown over time? **35**

True Statistics........... **44**

Resources **45**

Important Words........ **46**

Index **47**

About the Author........ **48**

Citrus fruits

Eating a healthy snack such as fruit is a great way to recharge after playing sports.

CHAPTER 1

The Right Food

Soccer practice was finally over. Daniel grabbed some chips and walked off the field with Max.

"Did you see Marcy score those goals today?" Daniel asked. "She was like a superhero!"

Max agreed. "She's been eating lots of nuts, fruits, veggies, and other healthy food. The food helps her keep up plenty of energy."

"Are you saying that zucchini and tomatoes help her score goals?" Daniel asked.

"Exactly," said Max, taking an apple from his backpack.

Fruits and vegetables are an important part of any healthy diet.

"Tyrone told me he stopped drinking soda," Max continued. "Now he says he feels better. He has an easier time paying attention in class, and he concentrates better on assignments and tests. He even got an A on our last math test."

"Marcy played really well, and Tyrone is doing better in school," Daniel agreed. "But I just don't see what food has to do with it."

Max smiled. "Try eating healthier and you'll see the difference for yourself," he replied.

Fuel for Your Body and Mind

The things you eat and drink have a big effect on the way you feel. A healthy diet can make you stronger and give you more energy. It can also help you think quickly and learn new things. Eating the right foods can even keep you from getting sick and make your hair and skin look better.

Instead of eating anything that looks tasty, think about how healthy the food is.

CHAPTER 2

The Building Blocks of Food

All foods contain substances called **nutrients**. These are the materials your body needs to work correctly. They are organized into six main groups—carbohydrates, fats, proteins, vitamins, minerals, and water. Understanding which nutrients are found in which foods is an important part of staying healthy. It will help you plan a balanced diet and avoid unhealthy foods.

When you eat healthy, you help your family and friends eat healthy.

Eating healthy complex carbs before playing sports or exercising will give you more energy.

Carbohydrates

Carbohydrates, or carbs, are the body's main source of energy. There are two kinds, called simple carbs and complex carbs. Simple carbs give you energy quickly, but this energy doesn't last long. Complex carbs keep you full and energized for a much longer time. Healthy eaters try to limit the amount of simple carbs they eat. Complex carbs are a much better choice.

Simple carbs usually come from foods containing **refined** grains and sugar. These include soda, candy, chips, white bread, and cookies. It is best to eat these foods once in a while, not every day.

Eat whole grain foods such as brown rice, oatmeal, or popcorn for complex carbs. These foods use the whole grain kernel, which contains **fiber**. Fiber moves food through your body. There are also complex carbs in potatoes, beans, fruits, and milk.

Breakfast is a terrific time to eat healthy carbohydrates. You get a powerful start from eating oatmeal or whole grain toast in the morning.

Fats

Despite their name, fats won't necessarily make you gain weight. They are an important part of a healthy diet. Fats give you energy. Your body stores them away for later. Fats also help you have

healthy skin. There are three main kinds of fat: unsaturated, saturated, and trans. Seek out foods with unsaturated fat. A little saturated fat is also OK. However, avoid trans fat entirely.

Adding olive oil to a vegetable dish is a great way to eat healthy fat.

A ripe, creamy avocado is rich with healthy fat.

One of the best sources of healthy, unsaturated fat is fish. Nuts, avocados, and sunflower seeds are good choices, too. Some cooking oils, such as olive oil and canola oil, are also packed with unsaturated fat. Saturated fat comes mainly from meat and dairy products. This means you should not eat foods such as butter and cheese too often. Trans fats are usually found only in certain **processed** foods. Avoid them as much as you can!

Proteins

Proteins are the building blocks of your body. Your muscles, skin, hair, and nails are all mainly made of protein. So are internal organs such as your heart. This means your body needs plenty of protein to grow. Proteins also help your body heal when you get a bruise or a scratch.

All meats are high in protein.

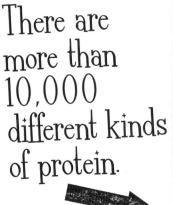

There are more than 10,000 different kinds of protein.

Tofu is a protein-rich food made from soybeans.

Like humans, the bodies of animals are made mostly of protein. This means animal-based foods can be a good source of protein for your diet. Chicken, beef, fish, pork, and other meats contain a lot of protein. So do eggs and dairy products such as milk or cheese. Not all protein comes from animals, though. Nuts, seeds, and beans are packed with this nutrient. So are foods made from these ingredients, such as tofu or peanut butter.

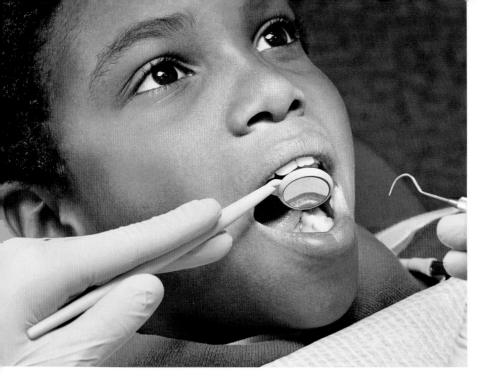

Vitamins play a major role in keeping your teeth healthy.

Vitamins

Vitamins help your body grow and stay healthy. Each one serves several important purposes. For example, vitamin C helps you see, fights off sickness, and heals injuries. Vitamin D helps keep your bones and teeth strong. Vitamin K helps you stop bleeding if you get a cut or scrape. Vitamin A is good for your eyesight and helps your body fight germs.

Different vitamins can be found in almost any food you can think of. There is vitamin C in citrus fruit, strawberries, and tomatoes. There is vitamin D in fish and eggs. Vitamin K is found in milk, broccoli, and leafy greens. You can get vitamin A from milk, eggs, and carrots. There are many vitamins. Eating a variety of foods is the best way to make sure you get them all.

Citrus fruits include oranges, lemons, limes, and grapefruit.

Minerals

Like vitamins, minerals are building blocks that help your body work. For example, calcium is a very important mineral that builds bones and teeth. You can get it from foods such as milk, broccoli, or salmon. Your muscles need a mineral called potassium. You can get it from potatoes, beans, tomatoes, and other foods. Other important minerals include iron, zinc, and magnesium.

A meal of grilled salmon and vegetables provides a variety of important nutrients.

All About Water

One of the most important parts of staying healthy is making sure you get plenty of water. Believe it or not, you could actually survive longer without food than without water. You need water to help nutrients move through your body and avoid **dehydration**. The best way to add water to your diet is simply to drink it whenever you are thirsty. There is water in drinks such as juice and soda. But it is much healthier to drink water by itself. You can also get water from fruits, vegetables, and many other foods.

All Day

Here are some ideas for simple, healthy meals. Use them to get started on the path to a healthy diet.

BREAKFAST

Try starting your day with oatmeal. This warm cereal contains plenty of carbohydrates so you'll have energy all day. It also contains protein, vitamins, and minerals. You can add all kinds of healthy toppings. Cinnamon, fruit, and nuts are good choices. Eat some fruit and drink a glass of milk to complete the meal.

LUNCH

Start with leafy greens such as spinach, lettuce, and kale. Add peppers, carrots, and other colorful veggies. Chicken, cottage cheese, or tofu will add protein and fat. Now add a bit of salad dressing, such as a mix of olive oil and vinegar or lemon juice. Have a whole wheat roll on the side for carbs. Enjoy your salad with a glass of water or unsweetened iced tea.

DESSERT

If you want a healthy dessert, try some fruit and yogurt. They taste great together! You could also have a small piece of dark chocolate. This sweet treat contains many important minerals.

DINNER

Baked chicken or fish are perfect, protein-filled dishes for dinnertime. Be sure to add steamed or roasted veggies. Brussels sprouts, broccoli, and cauliflower are all good choices. Round out your plate with a healthy grain such as brown rice. Your favorite spices and herbs are a healthy way to add flavor.

SNACKS

Snacks help fill you up between meals. Raw fruits and veggies are always a good snack. You can also spread peanut butter on apple or banana slices. Frozen grapes make a crunchy, cool snack. You can also have a muffin or some milk. Raisins, peanuts, and pretzels make a terrific trail mix.

CHAPTER 3

Making Healthy Choices

With the huge variety of foods available in grocery stores and restaurants, it can be hard to make the healthiest choices all the time. How much should you eat? Which foods should you avoid? How do you know what ingredients are in your favorite foods? The questions might seem overwhelming. However, the answers are simpler than you might think.

Choosing the right foods at the grocery store is the first step to eating healthy at home.

What Are Calories?

Almost everything you eat or drink has **calories**. Calories are a measure of the energy you get from food. You use this energy to play soccer, ride bikes, and swim. Some people need more calories than others. Someone who is small or not very active may need only 1,200 calories in a day. A larger, more active person may need more than 3,000 calories. Professional athletes and bodybuilders might burn more than 10,000 calories in a day!

You need calories to ride your bike or do any other kind of exercise.

Your body burns calories very slowly when you don't move around.

The more you eat, the more calories you put into your body. This means it is possible to eat more calories than your body can use. These extra calories stay in your body. They can make you overweight or even **obese**. Being obese can make it hard to move around and get exercise. It can also lead to other health problems.

Some foods, such as vegetables, are high in nutrients and low in calories. Others, such as packaged cookies, are low in nutrients and high in calories. This is why it is important to choose your foods carefully. You can use MyPlate (see page 29) for help knowing how much and what kinds of food to eat.

Dessert foods tend to be extremely high in calories, so it is best to limit how much you eat.

MyPlate

Nutrition can be complicated. Choosing the right foods might seem difficult at first. If you aren't sure what to eat, the U.S. Department of Agriculture's MyPlate food guide is a terrific place to start. MyPlate puts foods into five groups—vegetables, fruits, grains, protein, and dairy. It also shows how much of each group you should include in a meal. Visit the Web site on page 45 to learn more about MyPlate.

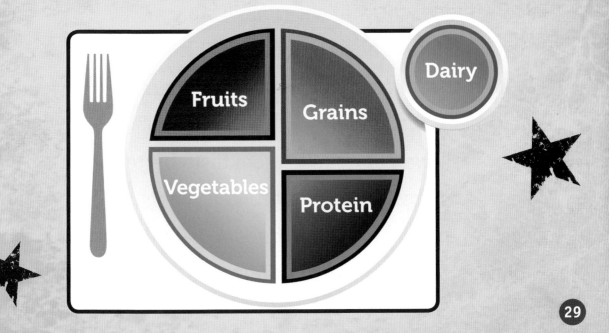

Most foods that come in boxes, cans, or jars have been processed.

Avoiding Processed Food

Many foods you find in a grocery store or restaurant have been processed. This means they were made in factories. The original ingredients have been changed in some way. They may also have **additives** that make them taste better or keep them fresh. Packaged cereals, chips, and cookies are all processed foods. So are most things that come canned or frozen.

These foods are often inexpensive. They are easy and quick to prepare. This can make them very tempting. However, while processed foods are not always bad for you, they are usually less healthy than fresh foods. They are often high in calories compared to foods made from fresh ingredients. Also, processing often removes important nutrients from ingredients.

Processed cookies are made using grain, but they do not have the nutrients found in whole grain foods.

Successful Shopping

Be careful when you're grocery shopping. You may want to buy a box of cereal, for example. Some kinds of cereal are very healthy. Others are not. Work with an adult to check the ingredient list and nutrition facts on the package. The healthiest cereal has less sugar and more fiber than others. Compare the labels of any food you buy to make the healthiest decisions.

Nutrition Facts
Serving Size 1 Box (34g)

Amount Per Serving
Calories 130 Calories from Fat 0

	% Daily Value*
Total Fat 0g	0%
Saturated Fat 0g	0%
Trans Fat 0g	
Cholesterol 0mg	0%
Sodium 170mg	7%
Total Carbohydrate 30g	10%
Dietary Fiber less than 1g	3%
Sugars 12g	
Protein 2g	

Vitamin A	10%	Vitamin C	10%
Calcium	0%	Iron	25%
Vitamin D	10%	Thiamin	25%
Riboflavin	25%	Niacin	25%
Vitamin B6	25%	Folic Acid	25%
Vitamin B12	25%		

* Percent Daily Values are based on a 2,000 calorie diet. Your daily values may be higher or lower depending on your calorie needs:

	Calories	2,000	2,500
Total Fat	Less than	65g	80g
Sat. Fat	Less than	20g	25g
Cholesterol	Less than	300mg	300mg
Sodium	Less than	2,400mg	2,400mg
Total Carbohydrate		300g	375g
Dietary Fiber		25g	30g

Nutrition Facts
Serving Size 1 Box (27g)

Amount Per Serving
Calories 100 Calories from Fat 10

	% Daily Value*
Total Fat 1g	2%
Saturated Fat 0.5g	3%
Trans Fat 0g	
Cholesterol 0mg	0%
Sodium 125mg	5%
Total Carbohydrate 24g	8%
Dietary Fiber 3g	10%
Sugars 12g	
Protein 1g	

Vitamin A	8%	Vitamin C	20%
Calcium	0%	Iron	20%
Vitamin D	8%	Thiamin	20%
Riboflavin	20%	Niacin	20%
Vitamin B6	20%	Folic Acid	20%
Vitamin B12	20%	Zinc	8%

* Percent Daily Values are based on a 2,000 calorie diet. Your daily values may be higher or lower depending on your calorie needs:

	Calories	2,000	2,500
Total Fat	Less than	65g	80g
Sat. Fat	Less than	20g	25g
Cholesterol	Less than	300mg	300mg
Sodium	Less than	2,400mg	2,400mg
Total Carbohydrate		300g	375g
Dietary Fiber		25g	30g

Nutrition Facts
Serving Size 1 Box (39g)

Amount Per Serving
Calories 150 Calories from Fat 10

	% Daily Value*
Total Fat 1g	2%
Saturated Fat 1g	5%
Trans Fat 0g	
Cholesterol 0mg	0%
Sodium 170mg	7%
Total Carbohydrate 34g	11%
Dietary Fiber less than 1g	2%
Sugars 15g	
Protein 2g	

Vitamin A	30%	Vitamin C	30%
Calcium	4%	Iron	30%
Vitamin D	15%	Vitamin E	30%
Thiamin	30%	Riboflavin	30%
Niacin	30%	Vitamin B6	30%
Folic Acid	30%	Vitamin B12	30%
Zinc	10%		

* Percent Daily Values are based on a 2,000 calorie diet. Your daily values may be higher or lower depending on your calorie needs:

	Calories	2,000	2,500
Total Fat	Less than	65g	80g
Sat. Fat	Less than	20g	25g
Cholesterol	Less than	300mg	300mg
Sodium	Less than	2,400mg	2,400mg
Total Carbohydrate		300g	375g
Dietary Fiber		25g	30g

Nutrition Facts
Serving Size 1 Box (27g)

Amount Per Serving
Calories 100 Calories from Fat 0

	% Daily Value*
Total Fat 0g	0%
Saturated Fat 0g	0%
Trans Fat 0g	
Cholesterol 0mg	0%
Sodium 95mg	4%
Total Carbohydrate 24g	8%
Dietary Fiber 2g	9%
Sugars 8g	
Protein 1g	

Vitamin A	8%	Vitamin C	8%
Calcium	0%	Iron	8%
Vitamin D	8%	Thiamin	20%
Riboflavin	20%	Niacin	20%
Vitamin B6	20%	Folic Acid	20%
Vitamin B12	20%	Zinc	8%

* Percent Daily Values are based on a 2,000 calorie diet. Your daily values may be higher or lower depending on your calorie needs:

	Calories	2,000	2,500
Total Fat	Less than	65g	80g
Sat. Fat	Less than	20g	25g
Cholesterol	Less than	300mg	300mg
Sodium	Less than	2,400mg	2,400mg
Total Carbohydrate		300g	375g
Dietary Fiber		25g	30g

The nutrition facts on food packaging show how many calories and nutrients are found in each serving of food.

Pizza night can be part of a healthy diet as long as you are careful about the other meals you eat.

A Little Bit Goes a Long Way

Just because a food isn't very healthy doesn't mean you can never eat it. It is okay to enjoy foods such as ice cream, candy, chips, or pizza once in a while. Think of them as special treats. As long as most of your meals are healthy, small servings of less healthy foods won't hurt you. Just be sure to avoid making them a regular part of your diet.

CHAPTER 4

The Science of Healthy Eating

Our knowledge of healthy eating practices has changed over time. In ancient Rome, people thought eating cabbage would cure illness. In ancient Egypt, people ate onions to sleep better. The first nutrition experiment did not take place until the 1700s. At this time, sailors at sea often came down with an illness called scurvy. Their gums bled and their teeth fell out. They felt worn out and sometimes died.

 Poor nutrition made sailing on long journeys dangerous.

A Cure for Scurvy

In 1747, Scottish doctor James Lind looked for a cure for scurvy. He fed different foods to 12 sailors. Only the two sailors who ate oranges and lemons got well. Lind did not know how important his findings were. In the 1930s, vitamin C was discovered in these fruits. The lack of this vitamin was the cause of scurvy.

After James Lind's experiment, more than 40 years went by before sailors started bringing citrus fruits on ships.

Dr. James Lind cares for a patient with scurvy.

Studying the Stomach

In 1823, U.S. Army surgeon William Beaumont began a study of how foods break down. He was called to treat a man who had been shot in the stomach. The man had a large

William Beaumont's studies helped us understand what happens to food after we swallow it.

wound. Beaumont operated on him but could not close the hole. The man lived with Beaumont for the next 10 years. During this time, Beaumont watched how his stomach worked.

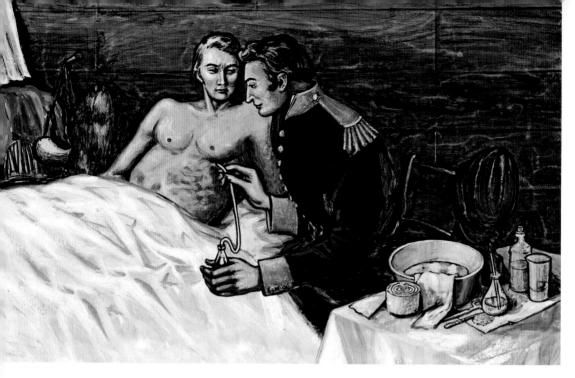

Dr. Beaumont inserts a tube into the hole in Alexis St. Martin's stomach.

Beaumont wanted to see how different kinds of foods broke down in the stomach. He tied strings around small food pieces. Then he dropped them into the man's marble-sized wound. Every hour, Beaumont pulled the food out, studied it, and put it back. He saw how stomach juices break foods apart. He also saw that certain foods take longer to break apart than others.

Atwater's Machine

In the early 1900s, American scientist Wilbur Olin Atwater studied how the body uses food. He built a machine that measured how much heat a person's body produced after eating different foods and then doing certain activities. This showed how much energy, or calories, the foods contained. Scientists now understood how much food was needed for daily living.

Wilbur Olin Atwater's machine helped us understand the effect calories have on the body.

Atwater's findings helped Olympic athletes learn how to eat healthier.

The 1900s

By the 20th century, it was known that spoiled food makes people sick. In 1906, the U.S. government began protecting people from unclean foods. Around the same time, scientists also began studying why certain foods keep people healthy. In 1912, Polish scientist Casimir Funk discovered certain materials in food that could cure sickness. He called them vitamins.

Timeline of Food and Health

1747
Dr. James Lind gives citrus fruits to sailors with scurvy.

1823
Dr. William Beaumont studies how food is broken down in the stomach.

Around the same time, Irish doctor Robert McCarrison began studying nutrition. His investigations continued into the 1930s. He thought many people got sick because so many nutrients were removed from food as they were being prepared for sale. McCarrison also argued vitamins were not the only substances in food that keep people healthy. Both of these ideas were found to be true, and today's **nutritionists** still agree.

1926–1936
Vitamins A, C, and D are discovered.

ChooseMyPlate.gov

(Dairy, Fruits, Grains, Vegetables, Protein)

2011
The U.S. government introduces the MyPlate food guide.

Early 1900s
Wilbur Olin Atwater figures out how much energy comes from different foods.

The government's dietary guidelines help determine which kinds of foods are served in school lunches.

Learning Healthy Habits

During the 20th century, the U.S. government started a variety of nutrition programs to help make sure children and adults got enough healthy food. However, different people and groups had different ideas about how to plan a healthy diet. In 1980, the government solved this by issuing its first official Dietary Guidelines for Americans. All U.S. food programs now follow this guide.

Food is a big part of our lives. It is important to find a balance between eating things because they taste good and eating them because they contain nutrients. But with all of the information we have about food and nutrition today, it is easier than ever to eat healthy. By simply paying more attention to what goes on your plate, you can be stronger and smarter than ever before! ★

What kinds of healthy meals will you eat?

True Statistics

Number of sailors who died from scurvy from 1500 to 1800: About 2 million

Amount of your body that is made up of water: About half

Length of time water stays in your stomach after you drink it: About 5 minutes

Calories the average American consumes per day: 2,544

Amount of pizza Americans eat: About 350 slices per second

Amount of meat the average American eats per year: 125 lbs. (56.7 kg)

Did you find the truth?

(T) Today's Olympic athletes eat healthy because of discoveries made in the 1900s.

(F) It is never healthy to eat fat.

Resources

Books

Burgan, Michael. *Food Engineering: From Concept to Consumer*. New York: Children's Press, 2016.

Butterworth, Chris. *How Did That Get in My Lunchbox? The Story of Food*. Somerville, MA: Candlewick Press, 2011.

Raatma, Lucia. *Making Smart Choices*. Danbury, CT: Children's Press, 2013.

Visit this Scholastic Web site for more information on healthy eating:
★ www.factsfornow.scholastic.com
Enter the keywords **Healthy Eating**

Important Words

additives (AD-uh-tivz) things that are added to foods during processing

calories (KAL-ur-eez) measurements of the amount of energy contained in food

dehydration (dee-hye-DRAY-shun) the state where there is not enough water in the body for it to function normally

fiber (FYE-bur) a part of fruits, vegetables, and grains that passes through the body but is not digested

nutrients (NOO-tree-uhnts) substances such as proteins, minerals, or vitamins that are needed by people, animals, and plants to stay strong and healthy

nutrition (noo-TRISH-uhn) the process by which the body makes use of food

nutritionists (noo-TRISH-uh-nists) scientists who study food and nutrition

obese (oh-BEES) extremely overweight in a way that is not healthy

processed (PRAH-sesd) prepared or changed by a series of steps

refined (ri-FINED) processed in order to remove certain substances

Index

Page numbers in **bold** indicate illustrations.

additives, 30
animal-based foods. *See* meats.
avocados, **15**

beans, 13, 17, 19, 20
brain, 8, 9, 14
breakfast, **13**, **22**

calcium, 20
calories, **26–28**, 31, **32**, 39
carbohydrates, 11, **12–13**
citrus, **19**, **36**, **40**
complex carbs, **12**, 13

dairy products, 15, 17, 29
dehydration, 21
desserts, **23**, **28**
dietary guidelines, 29, **42**
dinner, **23**, **33**

energy, 7, 9, **12**, 14, 18, 22, 26, 39, 41
exercise, **26**, 27

fats, 11, **14–15**, 22
fish, 15, 17, 19, 23
fruits, **6**, 7, **8**, 13, **19**, 21, 22, **23**, 29, **36**, **40**

grains, **13**, 29, **31**

ingredients, 17, 30, 31, 32

lunch, **22**, **42**

meats, 15, **16**, 17, 19
minerals, 11, **20**, 22, 23
MyPlate food guide, **29**, **41**

nutrients, 11, 28, **31**, **32**, 41
nutrition, 29, **32**, 35, 41
nutritionists, 41
nuts, 7, 15, 17, 22, 23, 32

obesity, 27
olive oil, **14**, 15, 22

potassium, 20
processed foods, 15, **30–31**, 41
proteins, 11, **16–17**, 22, 23, 29

refined foods, 13

saturated fats, 14, 15
scurvy, **34**, 35, **36**, **40**
seeds, 17
servings, 12, 28, **32**, 33
shopping, **24**, 25, **30**, **32**
simple carbs, 12, 13
snacks, **6**, **23**
sports, **6**, 7–8, **12**, 39
stomach, 37–38, **40**

teeth, **18**, 20, 35
tofu, **17**, 22, 23
trans fats, 14, 15
treats, 23, **33**

unsaturated fats, 14, 15

vegetables, 7, **8**, **14**, **20**, 21, 22, 23, 28, 29
vitamins, 11, **18**–19, 22, 36, 40, 41

water, 11, **21**, 22
whole grain foods, **13**, **31**

About the Author

Jane Sieving Pelkki is a registered dietitian and has a master's degree in public health. She especially likes to teach children how to cook and enjoy healthy eating. Pelkki has written many

newspaper articles for parents. This is her first book for children. She lives with her husband, Matthew, and their son, Sam, in Monticello, Arkansas.